Pause a Minute

With

Daphne Taylor

By Daphne Taylor

Writers Exchange E-Publishing

http://www.writers-exchange.com

Preface

I have here used the Australian Grass Tree as background for these 'Pause a Minute' thoughts. There are so many growing on "Tarkarendi", especially in inaccessible places. Each season I watch them and am fascinated by them and the life lessons they can be seen to exemplify.

They certainly do not rush in their growing. They have great resilience in their own environment, in good seasons or in bad.

When fire attacks, they erupt into furious fireworks - a veritable kaleidoscope of sparks - as the flame catches the long, cylindrical leaves.

But when the fire passes, leaving blackened trunks, they recover - in the Spring, again sending up the tight cluster of spikes, which as Summer unfolds, separate, to form a perfect shimmering sphere, glowing in the Summer sun. Brushed by animals, buffeted by wind, the leaves return to their appointed place in the sphere.

In good times of your life, may you glow where you are; when storms of life attack, may you return to your 'place' and in the longevity of years, may you endure, scarred but upright, like the Grass Tree.

PAUSE A MINUTE

I often hear a bird, commonly called the storm bird. His call fascinates me. He seems to be saying, "Come on, come on." Like a child calling urgently and persistently to his companions to come and play, to run free in delight and laughter, "Come on, come on."

Jesus calls, "Come on. Come on." Urgently, persistently He calls, anxious to take us in fun and joy. He knows the way for us to find happiness and full enjoyment. He IS the way. "Come with me," he says. "Let me lead you, be my playmate, my companion. Play the game my way. I'll take you safely home to our father. He will welcome you and you will know love. There will be rejoicing because we have come. We'll all be happy together."

So, often we take our own way, though we don't really know how to play the game. We play it our own way, make our own rules, and we get lost and the game is not interesting, leads nowhere, isn't fun at all.

Sometimes we think nobody cares, nobody wants to share our life and we feel alone, unloved, unwanted.

But Jesus is always there calling, "Come on. Come on." It is never too late. He's always ready.

It's just up to us to answer his call.

"Come on."

2. PAUSE A MINUTE

I was in hospital and feeling very drained, with the pain accompanying surgery. One day my daughter arrived with nail clippers and oil to see me. She rubbed my legs, cut my toenails and massaged my feet gently with oil. I soaked up the soothing treatment and was so relaxed by the time she finished I was almost purring. The touch of love.

Jesus touched people with love.

Think what it must have meant to the leper - an untouchable person, who most likely hadn't felt the touch of another human being for years - when Jesus touched him and healed him.

Think what it meant to the blind man when Jesus touched him and smoothed the spittle mud on his eyes.

Think what it must have been like when He took Jirus's little daughter by the hand, and said "Little maid, I say unto you, arise!" and the little dead girl was restored to her parents.

Jesus IS LOVE.

Touch someone with love today.

3. PAUSE A MINUTE

What variety of designs there are in Christmas cards! Many show three figures in long flowing robes, sometimes wearing crowns, sometimes riding camels, but always carrying gifts. The Magi, or three wise men. Men from the East who set out on a long journey over several continents - on a quest - to bring specific gifts to a child who was to be born. They had no proof. They had prophecies and the results of their study; and this they put to use to find the child and present their gifts - gifts for specific purposes.

This Christmas follow the wise men. Set out in search of Jesus; to find and really know Him and present your gifts.

Don't say you haven't any. We all have gifts.

Find them and present them

And you'll be surprised what will happen.

4. PAUSE A MINUTE

An eminent artist stated he was an agnostic. One who believes God is unknowable. Yet, this man was obviously a gentle spiritual man, with a firm belief in a God who is the source of all life. Creator. Great architect. Master painter of all beauty.

Is God unknowable?

Christians believe that at a particular time in history, God came to earth in the form of a human being. To live amongst us. To show us what God is like. To show us how to live with God and each other. And eventually to pay the price of death for our sins.

This was Jesus Christ. We believe, God in the flesh. God became for a space of time, for the twinkling of an eye - man.

When we look at Jesus, when we listen to Him, when we read what He did, we see and understand something of what God is like.

Do you believe this? Deep down?

Because this is what Christmas is all about.

5. PAUSE A MINUTE

Christmas is a time everyone observes - those who follow the Christian faith - those who give it lip service - those who are indifferent to religion - even those in countries of Hindu and Buddhist practice. It is big business in the commercial world. Yet, what is Christmas?

It is the celebration of the birth of a baby, who Christians believe was God in the flesh. Jesus. Mary's baby.

If that is true - God really came to earth as a human child - think what a risk He took. What if Mary had got tired of the constant demands of a little child and gone off to do her own thing? After all she was a teenager. What if Joseph had taken a fancy to another woman, perhaps nearer his own age? After all, this child wasn't his.

What if?

What if God needed a family, to come and live in and be cared for today?

6. PAUSE A MINUTE

INCARNATION

The world was sad, fearful and sinful
And man saw no hope for himself
Man had conquered his fellow man
And burdened him under a lash
Power and might were all esteemed
And the place of Love was a void

But Love brooded over the fettered world
And longed to set man free
And gather him under his sheltering wings
As a mother bird shelters her young.

But wayward man again and again
Turned away in selfish pride
Ignoring the warnings of visionary men --
So Love became a little child.

7. PAUSE A MINUTE

If you had the most wonderful news to tell the world -- you had found a cure for cancer, you could fix the ozone layer--and if you had limitless resources, power, money- how would you do it?

Would you employ a great speaker? Would you flash it around the world on radio or T.V.? Or use the best advertising company, the latest most super electronic technology?

When God had the news to tell, that He had come into the world as the baby Jesus Christ, He chose ordinary hard-working men. Shepherds.

And when 33 years later He had the news that Jesus had overcome death He chose ordinary hard working men and women -- fishermen, tax officials, house wives, mothers. Ordinary people like you and me.

Remember that this year as you think of Christmas.
TELL the NEWS! THE WORLD NEEDS TO KNOW.
CHRIST IS BORN.

8. PAUSE A MINUTE

At a certain time of year, spiders seem to appear from nowhere. A favourite place, easily overlooked is under the seats of my dining chairs. I become very conscious of the necessity to dust such places to eradicate danger.

New Year is a time when we need to take stock of our personal inner housekeeping - a time when we need to dust out, to wipe clean, the hidden parts so easily overlooked.

Have we allowed jealousy, greed, envy, hardness of heart, selfishness, to build up without being aware of it?

Have a good inner house clean. Get rid of the spiders and their webs.

Ask God's Holy Spirit to come in and fill your inner house with love, joy, peace, patience, kindness, gentleness - like a clean house filled with the perfume of beautiful flowers.

May the new year be a good, happy year for us all.

9. PAUSE A MINUTE

My little daughter came home from school all excited about the study of birds planned for the next day.

"We need a bird's nest," she said. "I said Daddy would get us one."

Of course it had to be an old one, and before such boundless confidence in his ability and willingness to procure such a nest, Daddy duly set out to search the creek banks with his own children and a troupe of the neighbourhood children in tow- and eventually arrived home with the needed item.

That's the sort of confidence we must have in our Heavenly Father. We must bring our needs to Him knowing He loves us, and desires our well being - knowing He will provide all our needs.

We should not come as cringing frightened outcasts, but as loved and precious children.

Jesus said, "When you pray, say 'Our Father'."

10. PAUSE A MINUTE

We once had a little bitsy puppy. She had the gentlest nature and most lovable ways but if she was left on her own for long, she got bored and then she got into mischief. Her chief misdeed was to grasp a pot-plant by the stem and shake or drag the pot around the yard. One such prized plant was in pieces, the pot broken and the soil scattered. We thought, "That's the end of that one."

However, some time later, after rain, up came that plant, multiplied, renewed.

God's bountiful goodness.

Sometimes lives are broken, scattered, and we think there is no hope of recovery or starting again. But with Jesus all things are possible. No life is too fractured, or torn apart, if we hand it over to Him, and trust and follow Him. From the debris, the mess, He will make New Life.

11. PAUSE A MINUTE

The whole business of sex, sexual attraction, sexual freedom, satisfaction, even sex discrimination, has possibly never been bandied about so freely as it is today by all ages. It is before our eyes and ears in one form or another in all the media. There is probably more knowledge on the subject available today than ever before. Even young children are surprisingly knowledgeable about their bodies and how life begins.

And yet there are so many broken marriages; so many single mothers; so many children being cared for, on a regular basis, by strangers in care centres of some kind.

When God came to earth as a baby, Jesus, He chose a girl, Mary, as the instrument of His birth. But He didn't only choose Mary. He also chose Joseph, the man to whom Mary was betrothed, a just man we are told, to care for and protect them.

Attraction between sexes is strong, but wisdom as well as knowledge is needed if we are to know and enjoy the wonders of true satisfaction and freedom within the love bond of marriage.

When we seek God's will about the person we are attracted to and make God central in our marriage, then we know true fulfilment.

12. PAUSE A MINUTE

When I was learning to drive a car, there was one thing I had to keep reminding myself. 'Keep your eyes on the direction you want to go. Don't look at the headlights or the dangers coming towards you. Or that is where you will end up.'

When I see the violence, the sordidness of some books, films and T.V. programmes, I fear for the people of our society. We see greed, jealousy, murder, fighting, deceit, immorality - not just suggested, but explicit. Presented in such a way as to appear acceptable, desirable, clever.

Is this where we want to go? The people of this country? These are things that lead to death. Death of an individual and of a country. These are the things that crucified Jesus.

What will take us in the direction we want to go, to fullness of life and growth? Things that are true, noble, courageous, pure, lovely, and honourable.

Where do you want to go?

To Death or Life?

13. PAUSE A MINUTE

One day I saw a cartoon - a small boy squatting down watching a tortoise labouring along. He was pointing at the tortoise and calling out, "Don't turtles ever get to go out and play?"

From a small boy's point of view, he saw the tortoise confined within his house, restricted, hemmed in, wherever he went, never able to throw off those restrictions and run free. He felt for the tortoise, all the frustration a child knows when for some reason he is couped up in the house for long periods.

We are often like that little boy saw the tortoise - restricted, hemmed in, carrying our burdens, whatever they may be, never able to throw them off and run free.

Yet, Jesus came to set us free. Free from the things that hold us down and prevent us from knowing fullness of life in harmony with God. He came that we should know forgiveness for whatever wrongs we may have done; whatever mistakes we may have made. He came to set us free to live in love.

We can be free if we trust Him, accept His love and follow His way.

Try it.

14. PAUSE A MINUTE

There's a series of quaint little cartoon like figures with the caption LOVE IS... No doubt you have seen them. Many bear thinking about. But what is love? How do we recognise Love?
    We are told in the bible,

> Love is patient and kind
> Love is not jealous or conceited or proud
> Love is not ill mannered or selfish
> Love is not happy with evil but is happy with the truth
> Love never gives up
> Its faith hope and patience never fail.

    Easter is all about Love. God's Love. Jesus died that we might go free. Our sins forgiven. At one with God.

    That's LOVE.

15. PAUSE A MINUTE

My friend and her little grandson were riding home from a pony club gymkhana. She had been one of the officials and the little boy a competitor. He'd had a lovely time and now sharing the ride home with his grandmother, his world was wonderful.

He looked across at her with love and said, "You know Marny, I hope you never die. I hope you live to be hundreds and hundreds of years old."

My friend was silent a moment, then she said, "Well, you know William, one day I will die, and when I do, I don't want you to be sad, because I'll be going to be with God and that will make me very happy. It will be very exciting."

William digested this thought for a few minutes then he said, "Alright Marny. I won't be sad. I'll say Whoopee!"

Can you be happy for someone you love, when they die - to go to be with God?

16. PAUSE A MINUTE

Many people today are very worried about the state of the world. Many young people see no hope for the future. Jesus once said, "Be of good cheer, I have overcome the world."

I cannot see how anyone who claims to be a Christian can be a pessimist. The Christian message, the gospel, the good news, is essentially optimistic. The world, or a great deal of it, is in a mess. Society is in a mess.

But GOD IS IN CONTROL.

Jesus rose from the dead. He overcame evil. His purpose will not be thwarted by Satan - or man under the spell of evil. It may appear for a time, that evil is all mighty because we have free-will, and God's patience is long. But the time will come.

This is GOD'S world.

Trust in God - follow Him - serve Him - and all will be well.

17. PAUSE A MINUTE

My friend's son got mixed up with drugs, and served a sentence for his involvement. My heart went out to her in her sorrow. She knew what was happening but could do nothing. He was weak and easily led and turned away from the teaching he had received. She suffered anguish.

Jesus wept over Jerusalem. When He came in sight of it in all its beauty, he wept that the people would not listen to Him and live by the will of God. He wept for them. He knew the consequences. Just as my friend knew the consequences for her son. But they went their own way. Did their own thing. Their own sin.

Jesus died for those sins. Those people.

He died for my friend's son. He died for you and me. Because we all go our own way. We all sin.

But Jesus overcame death and sin and He lives NOW. Our sins are wiped away. If we believe and trust in Him. We are free. Pardoned. Because of Him.

18. PAUSE A MINUTE

Have you ever suddenly, unexpectedly, met someone you love, when you thought them to be far away? A few days before my marriage, I was in the city making final preparations. I thought my beloved to be hundreds of miles away, when suddenly, there he was, walking towards me. My thrill of joy knew no bounds.

Imagine how Mary must have felt when she came to the tomb and found Jesus' body gone. She had seen him die on the cross. Now even his dead body was gone. Then someone she thought to be the gardener, spoke to her and she realised, here he was, here was Jesus - alive and talking to her. Nothing could have been further from her thoughts. Yet, here He was.

Jesus is always with us. In the most unexpected time and place, He is there. We know that joy, as we learn to recognise His presence - and that is possible for all of us.

Just ask Him to open your eyes.

19. PAUSE A MINUTE

Autumn is here. The days are becoming noticeably shorter, and we begin to think about the coming winter. Soon I must order a load of wood. Although the days are still hot, we prepare now for our well being when, as we know, winter will come. Summer may be long, and we may kid ourselves it will go on forever, but we know this is not so.

If we are honest, we know life itself does not go on forever. The day will come when we must face death. If we are wise, we prepare.

We thought a great deal about this over the Easter period. Because Jesus died and rose, came alive, death has no fears for Christians. Jesus passed through death and promises NOW, that if we believe and trust in Him, we too will pass through death to a new life.

As you prepare for winter, remember you need also to prepare for life - Life Eternal.

20. PAUSE A MINUTE

It's fascinating to weave a fabric, to watch the pattern emerge, the colours blend. It takes skills, patience, perseverance, and knowledge of what to do and what not to do, to produce a thing of quality. We need a pattern, a teacher, and when these things are combined with a real desire to succeed, then an article of beauty, usefulness and comfort is possible.

Life is like that - like weaving a length of fabric. If we want a life of quality, it takes patience and perseverance. It takes skills - skills in living harmoniously with others, at home or outside - in controlling our bodies, minds and emotions. It takes knowledge of how to go about it. If we have the desire, it is all possible.

In the Bible we have all the instructions necessary. We have the perfect pattern in Jesus.

And the Holy Spirit teaches and guides us if we ask. It's all there.

As we follow Jesus, it is all possible. Live a beautiful life.

21. PAUSE A MINUTE

A handicapped man said to me, "I want to ask you a question. When you are going to die, what does it feel like?"

Of course I replied, that I didn't really know what it felt like, because I hadn't died, had I?

He was feeling anxious, because in the home where he lived there had been three or four deaths of some of the really old residents, and he thought he might be next.

There is nothing to be afraid of in death. I couldn't tell him what it felt like but I told him I do know someone who died and came back to life and appeared and talked to many of His friends and He said, "I'm going to prepare a place for you."

That person was Jesus - God on earth. He's getting ready for our coming to welcome us.

Don't be afraid.

22. PAUSE A MINUTE

There were two things I used to do repeatedly, when I was a young wife. Two things that made a lot of difference to the taste of what I was cooking. And they were both things I forgot to add, things I left out of dishes. They were the sugar in the custard and salt in the porridge.

They are both pretty tasteless without those ingredients.

Life is like a dish. What you put into it determines what you get out of it - the enjoyment of it. If you leave out God, you leave out the sweetness, and life is uninteresting, like my custard - and you leave out the intensifier and seasoning, like the salt in my porridge.

It's always the right time to start a new dish, with God in your life.

It will be tastier and more enjoyable and exciting if you do.

23. PAUSE A MINUTE

My little four year old grand-daughter had just started answering the phone - but sometimes she forgot to say anything when she put the receiver to her ear. One day when I called, there was no voice - but I guessed she was there, so I said, "Hello."

Recognising my voice, the little answer came back, "Hello Nannie."

God is constantly calling us, but we often forget to answer. If we are not used to talking to Him, if His voice is not familiar, we may not even recognise it when He speaks to us.

Talk to Him in your own words. That's what prayer is - just talking to God, our Father. Ask Him to help you to recognise His voice, to answer when He calls. Make it a two-way conversation.

24. PAUSE A MINUTE

Do you have an opinion on the ordination of women? All and sundry have voiced opinions on this issue.

I came across this quote from a 17th century commentator on creation - man being made from dust - and woman from a rib from man.

"When God made woman, He did not take her out of man's head for her to lord it over him -
Nor out of his feet to be trampled on by him -
But out of his side to be equal with him -
From under his arm to be protected by him -
And from near his heart to be loved by him."

The article goes on to say that when Eve was tempted, Adam did nothing about helping her, and that when the Lord came looking for them in the garden, He didn't say first, "Eve what have you done?" He said to Adam, "Where are you?" He wasn't where he should have been when the devil tempted Eve.

Whatever your view on women priests, perhaps there is food for thought here on the responsibilities in spiritual matters - particularly the temptations in society today.

25. PAUSE A MINUTE

Many years ago, I made a little coffee table, with a mosaic top of broken pieces of tile. I covered this with a resin like substance to make it easy to wipe. However, this made it dull and dirty looking and it became sticky in the heat. It spoiled my beautiful table. I sought advice in removing it. I was told to chip it all off.

It took patience and perseverance to chip away around each little piece of tile but my design was restored to its beauty.

That is rather like our lives. God makes each of us beautiful with a purpose to fulfil. But we allow things to dull our beauty and spoil us for God's purpose for us.

BUT we can ask God to help us, to guide us. We can get help through His body, the church and although it takes effort, if we chip away bit by bit at that ugly exterior and shatter it away - the beauty will be still there underneath.

Have a look at your life and see if it needs some restoring to its full beauty and purpose.

26. PAUSE A MINUTE

Be Still.

This is an unfamiliar command in today's world. We are told 'hurry in for this - hurry before you miss out, time costs money - and we rush around at such a pace that we suffer from hyper-tension, stress, ulcers and so on, and we miss the peace - the little things - the lovely things that are all around us.

God says, "Be still and know that I am God."

The psalmist says, "He will lead me beside still waters,
He will refresh my soul,
and guide me in right pathways."
We all need that refreshment.

Take time to BE STILL. To Listen to God in your mind and in the sounds around you.

BE STILL and See God in His beautiful world.

BE STILL and Talk to Him, tell Him your innermost thoughts and feelings, your joys and your fears and hurts.

He Loves you. YOU are precious.

27. PAUSE A MINUTE

A man visited a friend in hospital. His friend was very despondent. His world was a gloomy place. All he could see was a black cloud of trouble and sickness. The man came away saying, "He's very low in spirit."

Another man met some friends who were bursting with the joy of life. He left them thinking, "My word! They are in high spirits."

What do we mean by this 'spirit'?

Christians believe in the Spirit of God. The Holy Spirit. God manifesting Himself in this way.

This is the power, which is the source of all life. It is energy, the invisible, intangible force that is in all and above all and through all - and without which the world and all in it, would be formless and void.

God the Holy Spirit gives us the strength, the courage, the energy, the wisdom and the will to cope with each day -no matter what our circumstances.

All we have to do is ask, trust and act on that trust.

May the Spirit of God be upon us.

28. PAUSE A MINUTE

One day during cold weather I had occasion to go into a certain shop. I had been miserably cold all day. In the shop it was so warm I looked around to see what form of heating was being used. The assistant told me that there was no heating system, it was just the warmth from the sun. A large glass door on the northern side, and the shop window to the west, caught the sun, and so it was beautifully warm inside.

So often we don't use this freely available power. We build walls where we should have windows to let that power in.

It's like that with the Holy Spirit. He is there with all the power necessary for our life. He is there to warm and comfort us. But so often we build walls between us and Him - walls of hardness of heart, selfishness, trying to do things in our own strength - and being cold and miserable. All we have to do is knock down those walls, open up our lives and hearts to Him and trust Him.

He gives us a warmth deep down inside.

29. PAUSE A MINUTE

A man had worked hard and long. He got into the habit of being always on demand, even when it was not really necessary and work became a burden. He retired and set about improving the home he had bought. Before long, he felt the garden must be watered, flowers picked, paths swept, the dog taken for a walk and the good habit of routine became a burden.

Sometimes we build high walls around ourselves so that we can't see the blue skies and the far horizons and we lose the joy of living.

Jesus came that we might have LIFE and have it abundantly.

Work is good for man - routine and efficiency are good - but if they shut out God's beautiful world and the joy of just being alive to lift up our hearts in praise…we need to look at our attitudes and our motivation.

God makes a beautiful new day every morning.

He wants us to enjoy it with Him.

30. PAUSE A MINUTE

A politician said to me, "You can't confront young people on a moral basis!" We were discussing some of the serious social issues of today. I disagreed with him. I believe many young - and older people - are looking for moral leadership and guidance from those in authority - in churches, educators or government - and I believe in a great many instances they are being sold very short in what they are given.

Are we afraid to take a stand today, for moral values? Are we afraid to speak up, where we are, in our daily life? Are we afraid of being laughed at, ridiculed because we believe and stand up for Christian principles?

The Holy Spirit is moving among peoples, moving in history, moving here in our own town but we must cooperate if we want to help stem the decline in our social standards, with its accompanying horrific diseases - the consequence of that decline.

It is not our young people who formulate Government policy, or advertising campaigns, or pornographic material.

Challenge your young people, yes, but challenge also those in positions of responsibility and seek the guidance, strength and wisdom of the Holy Spirit.

31. PAUSE A MINUTE

I once had surgery for the removal of a small part of my body, which was no longer doing its job, was causing me pain, and generally pulling down my whole system.

Jesus once said, "If your right hand offend you, cut it off."

Of course He was not really talking about our physical body but life. He wants us to have full abundant life. But sometimes there are things in our life that no longer fulfil their purpose, that bring us pain, unhappiness, things that hold us back, so that our life is not what God intends it to be.

I got a shock when I found I needed that surgery but I was told I would have new energy.

Examine your life, take an X-ray look at it, bring it to Jesus. Maybe you need some surgery too in your attitudes, your day-to-day living - so that you too can have new life.

May the Lord be with you.

32. PAUSE A MINUTE

My daughter once attended an evening class. One night, she arrived home to find her front door open, the rooms in chaos and the TV, video, stereo and micro-wave oven gone. It was very difficult explaining to her little daughter, what had happened.

"Where is the TV?"

"It's gone!"

"Well, go and get it!"

Simple to a little child. Not so simple when you don't know where it is, or where to look.

Some people feel like that when we talk about the Holy Spirit - about God. Maybe they have had some teaching in the Christian Faith but have lost what they had, and don't know where to look.

God is the most loving father we could possibly imagine who knows all about us, our difficulties, our trials, our potential and our dreams and desires, long before we ask.

Start by talking to Him, in your hearts and minds, in your own words -- join in with a group of worshipping people, a church, and ask for help in reading the Bible.

If you really want His company, He will meet you more than half way, as you take your first step.

He's calling you now.

33. PAUSE A MINUTE

I was choosing glass in a factory where stained glass windows are made. I had prepared my design for the window for the church, the donor had accepted it. I knew what I wanted. I held each piece up to see the effect when the light shone through it. I chose the colour, and noted the way the glass reacted as the light fell on the different facets of the textured pieces. It was difficult to find one piece I wanted - but the window was incomplete - not able to function or even hold together until each piece was put in place. Then it would be a thing of beauty, with a message to tell.

That is how it is with us. God has a design - a plan. He has made us each different - in colour, purpose, in gifts. He has a place, a purpose for each one of us without which His design is incomplete.

We are not all the highlight of the design - perhaps we are part of the background - but we are each of equal importance in His plan. The beauty and the function is marred if one piece is missing. The whole does not hold together as it is meant to.

Ask God to show you your place in His design - today.

34. PAUSE A MINUTE

One of our daughters used always to refer to anything unpleasant coming up as a dark cloud on her horizon. We all experience such things and the foreboding of the evil or unwelcome event overshadows all our thoughts and feelings. It has been so down the centuries.

This thought by Martin Luther King evinces the solution.

"When our days become dreary with low-hovering clouds
and our nights become darker than a thousand midnights,
let us remember that there is a great benign power in the universe
whose name is God and he is able to make a way out of no way,
and transform dark yesterdays into bright tomorrows."

May your tomorrows be filled with His glorious light.

35. PAUSE A MINUTE

As I entered the church, I admired a bowl of flowers on a stand near the sanctuary. They were a lovely soft yellow. How lucky the ladies were to find such flowers at this time of the year! Not till I was close enough to touch them, did I realise they were artificial. What a disappointment!

What is your Christian life like? What is my Christian witness like? Is it something beautiful, attractive to those in the church and those outside? Does it shine a beautiful colour for all to see? Has it a sweet perfume that delights all around? Is it soft and gentle to the touch? Is it full of life? Is it real?

Or is it like the bowl of artificial flowers - beautiful from a distance - but at close quarters hard, unresponsive, lifeless, nothing more than a show?

36. PAUSE A MINUTE

Homestead services of worship are a feature of Ministry in the West. The gatherings, sometimes on verandahs, sometimes on the lawn, are times of great family unity in the church and many moving times are experienced in the peace of the country.

At one such service, in the middle of the rector's sermon, we were joined on the lawn by the pet kangaroo. He loped gently into the circle, inspected each of the congregation, then moved over to the table being used as an altar. On his knees, he looked up to the wooden cross standing on the table, lifted his nose, and laid it at the base of the cross, his little front paws held simply before him. It looked as though he was begging for the sacrament.

My mind flashed to the kangaroo emblems, the huge model kangaroo used at the Commonwealth games - the kangaroo symbol of Australia. Was this symbolically Australia at the foot of the cross? Australia reaching out for the life giving body and blood of Christ?

It was a precious moment.

Pray God it was prophetic. For only thus will we all know dignity, peace and love; and freedom to develop and grow in understanding; and conserve this wonderful land we are lucky enough to enjoy and call 'home'.

37. PAUSE A MINUTE

A programme called "Share a Skill" was underway. A goodly group of ladies had turned up. Some were teaching, sharing their skills, others had come to learn. None were professionals. Some were teaching one skill and learning another. There was much discussion, many questions and answers, lots of enthusiasm and laughter in the good fellowship and the tentative attempts at new skills.

At the end of the session, one lady said, "We should have more time like this. We should make it longer, it's gone so quickly and we've run out of time."

That's how we should be in sharing our Christian faith with others, our knowledge and experience of putting that faith into action in daily life. Maybe we are not trained in theology, or teaching methods, but neither were my friends trained professionals in "Share a Skill". Yet they were willing to share the skills and knowledge they had developed.

Share your skills of living the Christian life with others, not by just talking about it, but showing them, step by step.

38. PAUSE A MINUTE

A Roman Governor once said, "What is Truth?"

What do you class as truth? When you fill in a government form? When you repeat something that happened at work or in your social group?

I once could have been granted a financial loan at a greatly reduced rate of interest, if, as was suggested, I had been willing to put not quite the truth.

What is truth?

Jesus said, "I am the Way, the Truth, and the Life!" The crystal clear, all light (no dark secret spots at all) - Truth.

If we have that sort of Truth in our lives, if our minds and souls are open to Him, then we have Jesus.

We are in the Way.

And we have Life.

39. PAUSE A MINUTE

My friend was worried about a little household situation.

"Pray about it," I said.

"Oh, it's not important enough to pray about," she said, though it was clearly bothering her.

Yet, you know Jesus was always interested in the ordinary things of life. When he healed Jairus' little daughter, he said, "Give her something to eat." He knew twelve year olds are always hungry. When the wine ran out at a wedding, he changed water in the pots by the door into wine and saved the host great embarrassment.

He used ordinary things like salt and water to convey his meaning.

"You must be the salt of the earth."

"I will be to you living water."

He is to be found in the ordinary things.

When the men from Emaus invited him to a meal and to stay the night, it was as he said grace that they recognized him. When he cooked breakfast over a fire on the beach and they ate with him, they recognized him. Jesus is where we are. Look for him. The gift is in recognizing his presence. It is much easier if we know him and are used to talking to him.

40. PAUSE A MINUTE

A florist told me that the week before Mothers' Day is her busiest time of the year. So many people order flowers for Mother. This is all very nice. I too love to receive the beauty of flowers. But when I look at the community, I wonder, if in many cases, this loving thought is carried all the year through. Is there always the thought to chop the wood for Mum's winter fires? To clean the leaves from the gutter? To fix a leak? Or a dripping tap? To mow the lawn or dig the garden? The things that Mum sometimes finds hard to do?

If we love someone, we want to do something about it.

Jesus said, "If you love me, you will keep my commandments."

And what are they?

"Love God with all your heart and mind and strength and soul, and your neighbour as yourself."

41. PAUSE A MINUTE

My grandmother used to say, "The devil finds work for idle hands".

With our shorter working hours and labour saving devices, what are we doing with that extra time? Are we any better, happier, more fulfilled? More satisfied?

When we look at our society we see it is sick. Perhaps many of us are going in the wrong direction, filling that time with superficialities, things that have no real value, things that are transitory pleasures or excitements at best, and degrading and evil at worst.

We have all the time there is - 24 hours a day. What we do with each 24 hours is up to us.

St. Paul says, "Fill your minds with those things that are good and deserve praise, things that are true, noble, right, pure, lovely and honourable." This is God's way.

Follow his way and you will find peace and fulfilment.

42. PAUSE A MINUTE

We had a family celebration at the Roma Cultural Centre. I took advantage of a lull in proceedings to visit the ladies' room. On my way back, I heard voices and looked up not watching where I was going. I slipped, or tripped, and too late realised I was going to fall into the pond beneath the mural. I threw out my hand and was able to prevent a bad fall but could not prevent falling, to sit in the water, in my special occasion finery. I had been distracted by the voices and didn't watch were I was going.

Where are you going in life? Where are you headed? Are you watching where your life is headed? Or are you distracted by all sorts of things around you?

Turn up the lights and take a good hard look at your life - what you are doing, where you are going - or you may land in deeper water than I did, and you may not be able to prevent a hard fall - and maybe broken hearts.

Ask God to help. He knows all about it. If you trust Him he will help, because He loves you. He's just waiting to be asked.

43. PAUSE A MINUTE

We once had some Islander girls living with us. Some friends of theirs were accommodated at a hostel in Brisbane. The girls told me of one friend who was not doing well in her studies and was obviously disturbed. It was discovered she was terrified of pouri-pouri, an evil force with which she, or one of her family had been threatened.

Some of us may scoff at such things, but there are evil forces in the world many much more subtle than pouri-pouri. Sometimes, people, for a lark or a dare - those looking for excitement or those looking for comfort in bereavement - <u>can</u> get caught up in seances - mediums- and before they know it, are involved in a realm of forces they know nothing about and find themselves in a situation, a bind, they are powerless to break. There is a spiritual world, and it is extremely dangerous and foolhardy to dabble.

Christians believe in the Holy Spirit. Jesus overcame evil when He rose, after dying on the cross. Satan, the devil, evil, is conquered and has no power over those who believe and trust in Jesus Christ. And the Holy Spirit is with us all the time.

44. PAUSE A MINUTE

A peacock feather lay on my work-table. I was using it for reference in a design I was working on. The sun came out and shone on the feather. I marvelled at its beauty. I picked it up and turned it to watch the light at different angles. The colours ranged from emerald green to gold to bronze to cerise. They really glistened in the sun. Peacock blue, we say, and that is there, but there is so much more.

God is like the sun, as He shines into our lives. He brings out the beauty and helps us discover wonderful things we didn't know we possessed. He gives the peacock its beautiful colours, its variety, and harmony. He gives us beauty in our lives if we let Him in.

Take a look at your life - and let God show how beautiful it can really be.

45. PAUSE A MINUTE

We trundled the pump down to the creek, set it up on the stand, and with great pushing and pulling, connected up the pipes and lowered the weighted end into the water. Then pulled the cord to start the motor. No result. We pulled and pulled, but not a spark could we get. Because of good rain, we hadn't needed to use the pump for many months.

We decided to remove the spark plug and clean it. However this was impossible. We even bent the spanner trying to loosen it. It had seized, or corroded on, through lack of use, and now when we needed water, we could not get it.

It is sometimes like that for a Christian who knows the faith, has the machinery - the means - of keeping in touch with God but, through lack of use, finds when a time of necessity comes, he can't make that contact to receive what he needs.

God is still there but we need to keep in touch, to keep the spark coming.

Don't let your spark plug seize up.

46. PAUSE A MINUTE

My six-year-old granddaughter was going to have her first nurse of her new baby sister. Her father was keeping a protective hand by the baby.

"I can do it all myself Daddy," she said. "I can manage on my own." Daddy insisted he must help, and reluctantly, she agreed.

Aren't we like that? We think we can manage on our own. We don't want our Father's help, or even seek his guidance. But thankfully, our heavenly Father keeps his protective arm around us. On our own, we can run into all kinds of danger - dangers we don't see, or even anticipate - because we don't see the whole picture. We only know little parts of our life's plan.

Let God help. He's the most loving, all caring, protective Father we could possibly imagine. We really aren't <u>very big</u> - or wise.

Ask Him to help.

47. PAUSE A MINUTE

A young relative phoned me in great distress. Her husband's grandfather had just died and the long-standing animosity between his two children had flared up.

"There's just so much hatred, and hurt from years and years ago," she said.

How sad! And how destructive! Not only to the relationships within the family, but to the persons holding that grudge.

When we nurse a hurt, justified or not, it grows and spreads, and is like a cancer in our soul. It affects every part of our being - spiritual, mental, and physical.

The antidote, the cure, the preventive, is forgiveness. Forgiveness from the heart. Forgiveness sets us free. It heals not only relationships, but bodies.

Let those hurts, those injustices we all encounter, bounce off. Don't take them in and harbour them.

We pray, "forgive us our trespasses as we forgive those who trespass against us."

Jesus prayed for those who were nailing Him to the cross.

48. PAUSE A MINUTE

I was trying to restore a little table. It is just a little pine table, but it is precious to me, because it belonged to my grandmother. I used stripper to remover the layer upon layer of old paint and sanded it all down but the original stain went deep into the wood and some of this remained. It did not look like new when I finished - I didn't really want it to - but it is still something of beauty and function.

That is how it can be with our lives. No matter what our life has been, how old we are, how many layers of experience of wrong living, how rough and scarred our exterior, God can strip it all away if we allow Him. He may sometimes use drastic measures - bereavement, heart attack, financial ruin - but He can reveal the beautiful underneath. He will get back to the real person. The original stain may remain but He can restore us to beauty and purpose in His world. We are each precious because we belong to Him.

It's never too late.

49. PAUSE A MINUTE

Often when I wake in the morning, I look out through the branches of the trees to the sun shining on the tops of the mountains on the far side of the valley, tipping them with glowing gold.

My spirit lifts. I contemplate the day for a little while, then say to myself, "Well come on girl! Rise and Shine."

That reminds me of the old Sunday School hymn -

> *Jesus bids us shine with a pure clear light*
> *Like a little candle burning in the night*
> *In this world of darkness we must shine*
> *You in your small corner and I in mine.*

There's a lot of 'darkness' out there in the world.

How is my light? How is your light shining? Is it touching all around with a golden glow?

50. PAUSE A MINUTE

I remember how we sat together on the veranda in the evenings, in the half light; the kerosene lamp on the table in the room behind, casting flickering shadows on the walls and ceiling; the stars appearing in a darkening sky; and a rising moon sending its first long shafts of light across the valley.

Being the little one, I mostly listened while the adults talked, and with pearls of wisdom, solved the ills of the world. A time of peace, time to think, and time to listen to each other.

Have we in today's world of stress on time and motion - time means money - money means profits - profits mean bigger and better business - lost the luxury of listening to each other? Those with whom we work, those in our community, those in our own homes?

Wherever you are - listen to those around you today.

51. PAUSE A MINUTE

The drought was long. The creek dried up. I moved the pump to the dam. One day, I went down the hill with petrol to set about starting the pump. I filled the petrol tank, turned on the petrol lever and the choke, then bracing myself with a hand on the top of the pump, pulled the cord. Not a flutter. I tried again and again. Not a kick from the motor.

What now? The tank high on the hill would be getting low. What could I do? This whole thing just wasn't my thing. Suddenly I realised I had not turned on the power switch.

I switched it on, pulled that cord again, and away it went. Water filling the tank!

Sometimes my inner motor won't start. I fret and fume until I realise I haven't switched on to the source of power. That power that is the motivator, the strength of all my being, who sustains me day and night.

We've all got that switch. And the power is always there. He doesn't forget or fail.

Don't forget to turn yours on today.

52. PAUSE A MINUTE

There's a story I remember from long ago. It goes something like this:

The sun and the wind were arguing who was the strongest, the most powerful.

They looked down and saw a man with a coat on, walking along a road.

"We'll settle it," said the wind. "We'll see who can make that man down there take his coat off." The sun agreed.

The wind blew hard, sending a fierce gust of wind earthwards. The man did up his coat to the top button.

The wind tried again, adding icy blasts. The man turned up his collar and pulled his hat down over his ears, looking up at the sky and hastening his step.

Again the wind tried, using all his force. The man bent double, clutching his coat around him and started to run.

Now it was the sun's turn.

The sun shone bright shafts earthwards. Then man looked up, loosening his clutch on his coat.

The sun smiled his radiance lighting up the road. The man now walking calmly undid his coat.

The sun smiled widely and his radiance filled the valley with light and warmth. The man stopped. Put down his parcels and took his coat off.

How different is the moral in this story from the modern aggressive marketing attitudes and principles that not only are advocated and operate in business and many other areas of society, but spill over into human, even family relationships today?

It bears contemplation. Which gets the desired result? And which promotes harmony and warmth where we are?

--- E N D ---

Afterword

All of these Pause a Minute thoughts, have come about in one way or another, through my own personal experience. They are therefore very personal.

I grew up feeling very much part of a large extended family of early Australian pioneers. I have spent over 40 years in eight parishes in New South Wales and Queensland, where my husband Harry was rector. I have 4 daughters, 11 grandchildren, and 1 great grandson, and many friends.

So, I have a host of memories, relationships, incidents, anecdotes that give rise to thoughts such as depicted in PAUSE A MINUTE.

I first wrote (and presented) thoughts such as these, at the invitation of the Roma Ministers Fraternal, for one-minute spots on radio 4ZR Roma, in the 1980's. Later, I did the same for Family Radio in Brisbane.

These are simply little every day happenings that give rise to deeper thoughts.

Thank you to those who have expressed appreciation for *Pause a Minute* since its introduction in Kilcoy Community News. It is very encouraging and gladdens my heart. This collection in book form is the result.

If you enjoyed this author's book, then please place a review up at the site of purchase, and any social media sites you frequent!

You can find ALL our books up at Amazon at:
https://www.amazon.com/shop/writers_exchange

or on our website at:
https://www.writers-exchange.com

All our Poetry Anthologies:

https://www.writers-exchange.com/category/genres/anthology/poetry/

All our Christian Books:
https://www.writers-exchange.com/category/genres/christian/

All Daphne's Books:
https://www.writers-exchange.com/Daphne-Saxby-Taylor/

About the Author

Daphne Saxby Taylor has always loved to write, in childhood making up stories to amuse herself, and in teen years writing poetry. She has written news, plays, skits and hymns for parish purposes where her husband Harry was rector. The experience of being journalist/editor for country weekly newspapers made her realise the power of the printed word.

On retirement she wrote her first Australian Historical novels, inspired by stories of her ancestors, all early settlers in Australia. She still writes poetry and has published Easy Reader books for adults, Children's Picture Books, and books for new writers for use in her occasional seminars. In her Children's Picture Books she combines her writing and illustrating skills. She lives in the upper reaches of the Brisbane Valley, Queensland, Australia and has four daughters, eleven grandchildren and one great grandson.

"MARY ANNE" is her third Early Australian Historical Novel, and her first e-published Novel.

Her Novels are written under the name, Daphne Saxby Taylor - and her other works Daphne Taylor.

You can keep track of Daphne's other books on her author page:
https://www.writers-exchange.com/Daphne-Saxby-Taylor/

If you want to read more about novels by this author, they are listed on the following pages...

Christopher Cuthbert Caterpillar

{Children's Picture Book}

An unusual friendship exists between Christopher Cuthbert Caterpillar and Mervyn Magpie. Although Christopher has been warned attending Mervyn's birthday party will be dangerous, he's filled with bravado and insists he can take care of himself. Christopher learns a hard lesson that courage is admirable but sometimes doing what we want to isn't always the best thing for us.

Publisher: https://www.writers-exchange.com/christopher-cuthbert-caterpillar/

Amazon Ebook: https://amzn.to/49TYbxf

Mary Anne
{Historical: Australian}

In peaceful Hertfordshire of New South Wales in the mid-nineteenth century, a bored and reckless man who leads a swashbuckling life in the army of the East Indian Company is told by the overseer that a married man has more chance of gaining a pardon from the penal colony and being granted land.

Gentle Mary Anne becomes the unwitting wife of such a man, sold for a bottle of rum. With no other prospects, she takes her mother's advice to love and care for her husband and his children in hopes that loving a hard man consistently will bring about the happily-ever-after she longs for.

Publisher: https://www.writers-exchange.com/mary-anne/

Amazon: https://amzn.to/41UKJHu

Pause A Minute with Daphne Taylor
{Poetry/Christian}

When Daphne Taylor first shared her "Pause A Minute" spots on regional radio, listeners wrote in asking for more. Now those one-minute messages--rooted in Australia's wide skies, dusty pumps, veranda evenings, and outback worship--are gathered into a single volume. Each numbered meditation begins with the commonplace and ends with a gentle challenge: forgive, pray, serve, believe. Whether she is rescuing a grass tree after bush-fire or watching a hospital monitor beep through the night, Daphne finds a gospel thread and offers it, warm and unpretentious, to you. These pages invite you to slow down, think deeply, and walk on renewed--scarred perhaps, yet standing upright in Christ.
Publisher: https://www.writers-exchange.com/pause-a-minute/
Amazon: https://amzn.to/43tOXql

Wilhelmina
{Historical: Australian}

Wilhelmina Gerhardt's life changes with a single summons to the Grand-Ducal palace. The grand duchess offers patronage; even the ailing Chopin agrees to guide the gifted pianist. But the rumble of revolution grows, and Colonel Johann Gerhardt uproots his family for the unknown colony of New South Wales.

The sea voyage exacts a cruel toll. In raw, beautiful Hunter Valley country, Wilhelmina must nurse her father, steady her frightened mother, and build a future from eucalyptus boards and determination. Friendship with neighbouring landholder James Montgomery eases their start; love for cedar-getter Billy Foster anchors her. Yet every choice seems to push music further from her grasp.

Across floods, droughts, and Billy's brief descent into rum, Wilhelmina's melodies remain--played on a battered upright, scored by candlelight, treasured in secret. When gifted youngest daughter Beccy earns her own chance at the concert platform, the past and present touch in a single breathtaking moment, and Wilhelmina finally hears her song soar.

Wilhelmina is a richly textured tale of migration, resilience, and a mother's legacy--perfect for readers who cherish family sagas set against Australia's colonial frontier.

Publisher: https://www.writers-exchange.com/wilhelmina/
Amazon: https://amzn.to/4dTdLLy